Little Girl Lost

1992 - 1998

Stephanie Jacobson

Table of Contents

breezes   3
without you   4
moonlight starlight   5
fuck   6
together   7
insanity   8
savior of love   9
escape   10
flame to flicker   11
rescue me   12
free   13
just want to know   14
all alone   15
damned   16
dreamer   17
even though   18
don't ever think   21
no escape   22
regrets, one   23
regrets, two   24
amazing grace   25
she wants to believe   26
something you can't have   27
she loved him once   29
peace   30
numb   31
love   32
falling   33
sorrows   34
freedom   35
letting go   36
long way down   37
another dream   38

Table of Contents
(con't)

losing you	39
just once	40
while you were dancing	41
if	42
disappear	43
crash down	44
missing	45
insomnia	46
goodbye	47
you	48
broken trust	49
coffee house	50
wanting	51
greatest fear	52
bad guy	53
liar	54
worth it	55
six months	56
piece of me	57
fool	58
for you	59
what I did	60
ramblings	61
peace and quiet	62
mistake	63
safety	64
out of reach	65
fucking	66
lucky one	67
stable	68
share	69
i'm sorry	70
angel, too	71

breezes

As time goes by
And days grow old
I look back
To times untold
When we were young
When we were free
And a time
When we were in love
I held your hand
You kissed my lips
And we were one
But we drifted apart
On the breezes of life
Your eyes
Your smile
They'll never fade away
Although you're just a memory
Floating on the breezes
Of my mind

without you

Daylight creeps through
The open windows
Gently cascading your face
And I think
Of what you mean
To me
And all the love
You bring
To me
And I realize
That if you weren't here
For me to share
My hopes and fears
That I shall also
Disappear
For I have nothing
Without you

moonlight starlight

To look out my window
On a clear and starry night
And wish you were here
To keep me warm
But you're a million miles away
And as I think
Of your needed love
And look up at the stars above
The same moonlight
That illuminates my room
Reaches clear across the world
To do the same for you
Moonlight,
Starlight
It's all the same to me
As long as it's the same
Strong light
That guides you back to me

fuck

I don't give a fuck
About life anymore
Where you'll find me
I don't know
If I show you
How I feel
Will you live this life for me
Until the warm
Gentle grip
Of death
Claims my soul
And wraps around me tightly
Sealing off my last breath
And slowly
Slowly
I fade to black
And I'm finally at
Peace

together

As we grow together
You and I as one
We'll sail away together
To our place under
The sun
Never to return again
My love for you
Grows stronger
My heart beats faster
Every time you call my name
You
My love
Are the only one
Who makes me feel this way
You are my everything
My heart
My dreams
My soul
My love
Nothing compares to you
And nothing ever will

insanity

Insanity
All around
As I walk
The hallowed grounds
I was hell-borne
Into lunacy
Try to find
Security
In the land of
Chaotic dreams
Thoughts are cruel
From a lucid mind
Ripped at the seams
From this home of mine

savior of love

I'm alone
Washed upon the shore
A piece of debris
Floating on by
Waiting to find
My little lone island
Gasping for air
A gentle hand
To stroke my hair
Sweet lips that caress
Like a brisk ocean mist
Cast upon my face
I lay and relax
Sweet with your touch
You are my love
My gentle breeze
And a kiss will seal
Forever
Our love for
Each other
Throughout all time

escape

Feeling trapped
No way out
Trying to escape
This wretched life
But there's no
Way
Out
Just to wait
For death
And slowly die
Its presence
Seeping through my veins
Black
Cold
Death itself
Watching
Laughing
At my pain
Until there is
No more

flame to flicker

Darkness, dawning
All I see
Anything is nothingness
Surrounding me
Falling slowly under your spell
Flame to flicker, time will tell
I reach for my last sip of blood
Under eternal sleep I fall
Nothing but your name I call
Out for you
I need you now
Please rescue me
A glowing warmth fills my soul
A bittersweet pain fills my bloodshot eyes
Tears streaming down my face like blood
From an open wound
Cut deep into my soul
Sweet smell of whiskey filling up my mind
As I pull the trigger, as I flip the switch
Whisper good-bye, wish my last wish
Kiss you good-bye as you weave your spell
Flame to flicker, time will tell
Only god knows the answers
While you are laid to rest
Forever in your peaceful sleep
Good night
Good luck
Good bye

rescue me

I sit in the dark
A place to hide
No one can see me
Myself I cannot find
What I've been looking for
All my life
Nothing's been right
So why stay around
Till tomorrow?
Tis another day
Another way
To find myself
In my mind
Help me
Please
Rescue me

free

Found my rainbow
Behind the clouds
Followed it
For hours
Ended up on the
Other side
Nothing there for me to see
Except what I've been looking for
A land of peace and happiness
Of love and sanity
A place where I can run away to
And never be afraid again
And where I will always be loved
Always be me
Always be free

just want to know

I just want to know
What makes you tick
How you think
And how you feel
I just want to have
A life I can enjoy
Be myself
And feel what
I want to feel
All I want to know
Is what makes me love you
How you make me feel
The way you do
All I want to tell you
Is how I feel for you
And I just want to know
How we got this far
And I just want to be here
Safe in your arms
All I want to know
Is what makes you love me
How I make you feel
And all I want to hear you say
Is
I love you

all alone

As I sit
In the dark
By myself
All alone
I wander
Through life
In my mind
The chasm
So hollow
So cold
Alone
The abyss
The darkness
Shadows
And light
Cast upon stone walls
Play tricks with the mind
Confusion
Still alone in the dark
No one around
Yet still
Paranoid
Find a way out
Of this maze
We call
Life

damned

Damned for all time
In this life
Nothing's right
Look for tomorrow
When I can be free
Everything
Nothing
Always will be
Here with you
So close
Please leave
Holding all the answers
Tightly in thy grip
Cowering in the shadows
Hide away
Far away
Stay away
Look onward to tomorrow
Could this go on forever
Or will I be set free
Will tomorrow ever come
Or will I be trapped here
For eternity
Damned for all time

dreamer

I know I've met you before
Somewhere in my dreams
Hear your voice
Whispering through my window
Calling out my name
I dream at night
Being so close to you
Feeling so safe in your arms…

even though

How
BLACK
Everything is even though
My eyes are
OPEN
No
LIGHT
Around cannot make
Anything out
Feel
SCARED
Someone is watching
Watching my every
MOVE
Feel
ALONE
No one around
To protect me from
What lurks in the
DARK
How
QUIET
Everything is
Even though i
Am making
NOISE
No
SOUND
From anything
Even though they're
WATCHING
So I sit
STILL
Afraid to move

18

They may
STRIKE
Out at any time
And take me away
Pull me into
The dark
ABYSS
No one to save
Me how
NUMB
Everything is
Even though i
Try to
FEEL
My hand touches
Something
WARM
Is it
BLOOD?
From where does it seep?
From a deep
Gaping
Wound through
My
BODY
Slice
Cut
BLOOD
How
CALM
Everything is
Even though i
PANIC
I scream
No one hears
Because I am

ALONE
In the DARK
How
WARM
Everything is
Even though
I'm lying
FACE DOWN
In the
SNOW
How
GENTLE
Everything is
Even though
LIFE
Is rough
FEELS
Like being dragged
Over glass
SHARP
Cutting into your
Skin
Over and
Over
In the few precious
Moments of
LIGHT
I see Satan
Laughing
Laughing
Laughing

don't ever think

DON'T EVER THINK I DIDN'T LOVE YOU
Because I never said so
DON'T EVER THINK I DIDN'T WANT YOU
My feelings were never rushed
DON'T EVER THINK I DIDN'T NEED YOU
When I pushed you away
DON'T EVER THINK I DIDN'T LOVE YOU
You hold a very special place in my heart
DON'T EVER THINK OF LEAVING ME
Life would never be the same

no escape

Feeling trapped
No way out
Trying to escape
This wretched life
But there's no
Way
Out
Just to wait
For death
And slowly die
Its presence
Seeping through my veins
Black
Cold
Death itself
Stands before me
Watching
Laughing
At my pain
Until there is
No more

regrets, one

I wish I could have known you better
but I never had the chance
to tell you what you mean to me
through our wild-eyed romance
but your love slipped
right through my grip
and left me here alone
and I was left there
right by your side
left alone to mourn

I wish I could have know you better
But I never had the chance
To hold you close in my arms
And keep you safe from harm
But you lost your life
That dreadful night
When you tipped that bottle back
Again and again
Until the gentle hand of Death
Led you to his home
And you were gone
Like the bluebird's song
On a cold and cloudy day
Leaving me all alone
Leaving me to live my life without you

regrets, two

I should have been there with you
I should have tried to stop you
Before you were taken away
How was I to know
You'd never come home
That I'd only see you
Once again
So cold and pale
How foolish I was
To let you go
So many things I should've done
I should've said
But now it's too late
You're gone now
Nothing can change that

You should've know better
Should've pushed that bottle away
But you gave up
Surrendered
And let god take your soul
Now you're gone
And I'm all alone

But I know one thing
You're watching over me
Hoping the same mistake
Won't be made twice

amazing grace

They sang 'amazing grace' for you
They said how you loved and you laughed
While I sat and cried

I tried to comprehend everything

They sang 'amazing grace' for you
They talked of your life, your family
As I sat and cried
And slowly all my happiness died
And was laid before me in a suit and tie

I asked myself why and tried to comprehend everything

I sang 'amazing grace' for you
And read your tombstone through my tears
I talked of your life, your love
Knelt down and placed a single white rose
On your grave
Then said good-bye
And slowly
Slowly
Walked
Away

she wants to believe

She wants to believe
In fairy tales
The castle,
A princess
And her prince
She wants to believe
In herself
Her dreams,
Her fantasies
She wants to believe
She can do better
But she knows
She cannot
This is who she is
What she has to live with
There's no way to change it
She wants to believe
She can be saved
But she can't
It's too late

something you can't have

spinning in circles
confusion all around
dancing in a daydream
full of bright colors
she looks around
sees
purples
pinks
yellows
spots a soft red rose
with dew drops on its velvety petals
she reaches down
and is pricked by a thorn
she looks at her finger
slowly seeping blood
with a tear in her eye
she looks at the flower
in the distance
she hears a voice whisper
"that is something you can't have."
Walking in circles
confusion all around
wandering in a nightmare
full of darkness
she looks around
and sees
grays
blacks
blues
spots a white pieces of paper
with only one word on it
she reaches down to pick it up
and is cut by its sharp edge

once again
drawing blood from her finger
with a tear in her eye
she looks at the page
in the distance
she hears a voice whisper
"That is something you can't have."
Running in circles
Confusion all around
She looks around
and sees
in the distance
the man of her dreams
hugging another
she reaches to touch him
then sees them kiss
and her heart is shattered
by the sight
her eyes dripping
with tears
and with an emptiness in her heart
she looks at the happy couple
so in love
in the distance
she hears a voice whisper
"That is something you can't have."

she loved him once

She loved him once
She'll love him again
No matter how painful
Her heart feels
She will be his again

He loved her once
He'll love her again
As soon as he realizes
That pain he has caused
He will be hers again

They loved each other once
They'll love each other again
Once they realize they can't
Live without one another
They'll be together again

peace

Laying peacefully
In your arms
A blanket between
Our bodies
And the sand
Waves roll up
Tickling our feet
You pull me close
Our lips meet
Oh, sweet kiss

The setting sun
Glistening off the water
Dancing in your eyes
Your skin
So warm against mine
You brush my hair
Away from my face
While you gaze into my eyes
And draw me close
For a kiss
Oh, sweet kiss

numb

Left all alone
In the dark
Hurt
By your actions
And words
Of hate
Pain
Greed

love

Love
Is not as simple
As it may seem
Love
Is cruel
Heartless
It's the prick
Of a thorn
On a lovely red rose
And the salty tear
Of a broken heart

falling

Falling
From the edge
Of reality
Of normality
Drifting
In and out
Of consciousness
Grasping at straws
Gasping for breath
Trying to scream out
But my voice is suppressed

sorrows

I'm drowning in my own sorrows
Life is too short
And it goes by unnoticed
Until the very end
When the only words left to say are
"I wish I had done things differently"

freedom

Let's run away
Leave our lives behind
And start again
Somewhere new
Be free to be
What we want to be
Not worry about
Anyone or
Anything
And concentrate only on
Each other's love

letting go

What does it feel like to want someone
Someone you know
You can't ever have
But to want that someone so badly
It hurts
Hurts enough that you numb
Your body to feel nothing
And it shows no signs of letting go?

long way down

I finally felt my heart
Break last night
And I truly know what
It's like to be alone
I was on top of the world
It's a long way down from there
And I'm nowhere near
Strong enough
To make that climb back up again

another dream

I want to be back there
To be in your arms
Safe
Secure
You smell wonderfully
Nuzzling your neck...

losing you

Never has anything
Shaken this world
Than the thought
Of losing you
Before your time was due
I've never felt such sorrow
My feelings have become so intense
Life has become
So final
So cut and dry
Endless possibilities
Now have deadlines
And dreams are vanishing
Day by day
Prayers are now thought
To be unanswered

just once

How I've dreamed of holding you
touching you
loving you

Just once

To know how it feels
To be loved by you
The feel of your lips
your body next to mine

Just once

To know how it feels
to be held
in your arms
like a child

To run my fingers through your hair

To hear you whisper my name
To share your hopes
your dreams
your fears

Just once…

while you were dancing

While you were dancing
I stood there in the corner watching
Waiting
Wanting
Needing to be loved
Caressed
Held in your arms

While you were dancing
I sat at your table dreaming
Hoping
Daring to reach out to you
To feel you close
Your body pressed to mine

Even from here
I smell your cologne
I taste your sweet lips
Oh, how I wish
For one dance
With you

if

If I were to love another
Would you take me back
If it didn't work?

If I were to love another
But love you in heart and soul
Would I be forgiven?

If I were to love another
Would it be the same
As the way you love me?

disappear

All the world seems to disappear
As soon as I'm in your arms
I feel so safe
And secure
And loved
Like nothing in the world
Can harm me

crash down

Everything came crashing down
Falling
Tumbling
My whole world
Is falling apart
At the touch of a button
The world as we know it
Shall never return
It has been destroyed
With a cruel sense of reality
Playing endless mind games
And nothing ever becomes of it
The world as we know
This world stood still
Like it did so many times before
And I'll never be the same again

missing

God, what I wouldn't give
To be back in your arms again
To feel your warm breath on my neck
To taste your lips
Your kisses
Sweet, gentle
Soft kisses
My hands caressing your strong back
Holding you close
My fingers running through
Your soft golden hair
A passionate embrace
Where did we go wrong?
Is it hopeless to dream
That someday you and I
Will be together again?
And you'll be holding me in your arms
I'll feel your warm breath on my skin
Taste your sweet lips
Your kisses
Soft, gentle
Sweet kisses
My hands will caress your strong back
And I'll hold you close
Run my fingers through
Your soft golden hair
A passionate embrace

insomnia

Over and over
Again and again
As I try to make sense
Of this place
Just lie here in the dark
Sitting all alone
Waiting for someone to
Save me
Cannot find comfort
In this world
Talking to myself
It's 12 o'clock
Sleep never comes
No rest for the wicked
Just a prayer for the dying

good-bye

I don't want to deal with
Losing the life of a friend
I don't want to have to face
The fact that you
May not be there someday
And why does a friendship
Have to be threatened
With a finale
So soon after it started?
How do you deal with
Losing a friend
Not by anger or fighting
But by sorrow and death?
And what time
Do you give up
On faith and hope
And come to reality?

you

The scent of jasmine
Reminds me of the times
We spent over dinner
In your car
As we sat in the parking lot
Facing the highway
Watching the cars pass by
We could sit and talk for hours
About nothing and everything
And I thought we understood each other
You opened up to me
You were sincere
Honest
At least that's what I was lead to believe
You said you weren't good enough for me
I didn't want to believe you
And I still don't

broken trust

How is it
That you can live with yourself
After the lies you told me?
How can you be
Honest with yourself
If you can't be honest
With someone else?
How do you ever expect
To find yourself
When the real you is buried beneath
Deception?
And where you get the courage
To lie right to my face
Is beyond me
But it'll come back around
Someday
And you'll realize
Just what kind of person
You really are

coffee house

Endless chatter that blends in
Like background music
Snow blows by the window
Horizontally
The clank of coffee spoons
In their cups
Reminds me of a past love
Who rank a little coffee to go with his sugar
Sipping it sweetly out of his spoon
Soft, sweet hands playing
With empty creamers
Puling another cigarette
Out of the red and white pack
Those days are gone now
But the memories are still alive
In my heart
And in my mind
As I sit here
Sipping my coffee
Out of my spoon

wanting

What is it that you have
That no matter what
Still draws a part of me towards you?
You've got your hooks into my heart

You used my own damn feelings against me

But there's still too many little coincidences
For me to put this aside
Chalked up as a bad experience

greatest fear

My greatest fear
Has come true
And here I am
All alone
No one to comfort me
No one to love me
And here I am
All alone

the bad guy

I had to play the bad guy this time
I had to be the one
To break your heart
And not give a fuck
About your pain and suffering
Maybe you should
Shut up and stop feeling sorry for yourself

liar

You believed me when I said
I loved you
And all I did was lie
I was being used
And used you in return
To deal with my own pain
And pushed you away
As I was being pushed away
Leaving me nothing to live for
And I'm still here
Alone in the dark
Hoping and waiting
For the light

worth it

The affair was worth the pain
If it had never happened
I'd be even more miserable
You gave me a taste of
Happiness
Of freedom
Of peace of mind

six months

It's almost been six months
Since you and I
And I'm still unable to let you go
My life is infected
With the haunting memories of you
I spend every night
In a bed we once shared
And I can still smell you
Taste your sweet kisses
Feel your touch

piece of me

you took away a big piece of me
when you left so abruptly
if only you had explained
I thought you were sincere
In everything you told me
You left a deep gaping wound
Not yet ready to begin to heal

fool

Man was I a fool
I should've known better
Than to actually believe
That all my dreams
Were coming true
And happiness was near
All because of you
I should've known better
That good things never happen
To me
It was all just a dream
I'm just waking up from

for you

Everything I've ever done
I've done for you
But with no acknowledgment
No appreciation
Your words sound pretty and sincere
But your actions speak volumes
Of who you truly are
You fooled me into loving you
Blinding me with those things
I truly wanted
But you never gave a damn
And in one simple moment
My world was destroyed
Crushed by a hand I thought was kind
But it was just as cruel and ruthless
As I should have imagined
I should know better than to think
Good things happen
To people like me

what i did

What did I do
That was so horrible
So terrible
That you couldn't love me?
I played all of your
Egotistical games
I laughed at all of your jokes
Felt pain in your sorrows
You were able to be honest with me
At least that's what you said
So why was it
When I was honest with you
You shut me out of your life
With no warning
No explanation
No feeling
And you were the one
who was afraid of getting hurt

ramblings

I sit here
And write
And ramble
About nothing in general
But yet I'm releasing parts of my emotions
That are still trapped within
So I write
And I read the words on the page
And they seem to not make sense
But yet they make sense of everything
So I continue to sit
And write
And ramble
In the hopes that someday
Someone will read this and understand
The feelings
The heartbreak
And the pain
I've felt for years

peace and quiet

I don't understand
Why I just can't seem to have
Peace and quiet
I don't ask for much
Just a quiet spot for me to sit
And thing
And be alone
No one asks stupid questions
Annoying questions
No distractions
No interruptions
Just peace and quiet
A chance for me to be alone
Oh Christ, just shut the fuck up already!
You sit over there
Oblivious to your
Annoying antics
And you,
You wretched bitch
You wander around the room
Poking your nose into business
That doesn't involve you
And you have the audacity
To ask me what's wrong?
Just go the fuck away, would you?!

mistake

If we can get through this
We can get through anything
And what a learning experience
This has been
My world almost came crashing down
Around me
My safety net was cut
From beneath me
To almost think that the love we shared
Such beautiful, passionate romance
Almost destroyed this on one level
And brought us closer on another
To think that this love we shared
Almost created a new life
A life that would have never been
But just the thought of the two of us
Creating another life…
I hope to someday get the chance
To tell you the same thing
And this time let it be true…
And a welcome piece of news

safety

Hold me close
Keep me safe and warm
In your arms
Let me rest
My head on
Your chest
And listen to your
Heart beat
And fall asleep
With you

out of reach

My dear
It seems like forever
Since I've been here
And these feelings I've known
Many times before
Have become so new to me
I know not what I want
So I have yet to find a way
To get it
It seems to be right in front of me
Almost teasing
Taunting
Mocking me
All things come to those who wait
But how long must that wait be
Before happiness
Sweet, sweet happiness
Is mine

fucking

Dear god
The knowledge of
What I've missed out on
All these years
The unbridled raw passion
Pure animalistic
Carnal knowledge
Before now
Everything seems like it was
Sugar coated
When there's oh so much more
Like I've opened up
A whole new world

lucky one

How did I end up
Being so lucky
To have someone
As wonderful as you
Walk into my life
At just the right moment
Just when I needed
Someone to talk to
Someone who could understand
Where I was coming from
But you've given me
So much more
And for that
I am grateful

stable

You're such an important
Part of my life right now
When I'm with you
I feel at peace
And everything else in the world
Seems to disappear
Like we're the only ones around

share

Once again
I've been asked to share
My works for public ridicule
And this time I comply
Regretting the decision
From the start
I suppose it's lack of confidence
Or lack of talent
Either way…
Do I really need everyone
To read my words?
I've never written anything for anyone
Why should I do it now?
How are these words profound
And worthy of public consumption?
No one will walk away after reading this garbage
With a new outlook on things
They'll just wonder why they wasted their time
With such nonsense

i'm sorry

I'm sorry I can't make you love me anymore
I'm sorry you can't make you love me
I'm sorry I acted like such a jerk
I'm sorry you got pulled into this
Silly childhood game
And everything got so screwed up
I'm sorry you got sucked into her web
When you were in such a fragile state
I'm sorry I sent you into the arms of another
I'm sorry I, too, played along with the games
And let jealousy consume me
Eat away at me
Destroy me, destroy you, destroy us
I'm sorry we can't seem to be able
To pick up the pieces and
Put them back together

angel, too

I want to be your angel, too
I want to be romanced
Held in your arms
You were my savior
You were my everything
I thought I was yours
I held your heart so closely
Your touch was sweet and kind
Loving and thoughtful
Your hand enveloped my hand
When you held it
Pulled it close to you
And placed a soft, sweet kiss on it
You laid me down
On a bed of rose petals
And loved me
Once upon a time

www.ingramcontent.com/pod-product-compliance
Lightning Source LLC
Chambersburg PA
CBHW031331040426
42443CB00005B/290